PRO SPORTS
BIOGRAPHIES

AARON JUDGE

by Allan Morey

AMICUS | AMICUS INK

Amicus High Interest and Amicus Ink are published by Amicus
P.O. Box 1329, Mankato, MN 56002
www.amicuspublishing.us

Library of Congress Cataloging-in-Publication Data
Names: Morey, Allan, author.
Title: Aaron Judge / by Allan Morey.
Description: Mankato, Minnesota : Amicus ; Amicus Ink, [2020] | Series: Pro
  sport biographies | Audience: Grades: K to grade 3. | Includes
  bibliographical references and index.
Identifiers: LCCN 2018039455 (print) | LCCN 2019003685 (ebook) | ISBN
  9781681517445 (pdf) | ISBN 9781681516622 (library binding) | ISBN
  9781681524481 (pbk.) |
Subjects: LCSH: Judge, Aaron, 1992- —Juvenile literature. | Baseball
  players—United States—Biography—Juvenile literature.
Classification: LCC GV865.J83 (ebook) | LCC GV865.J83 M67 2020 (print) |
  DDC 796.357092 [B]—dc23
LC record available at https://lccn.loc.gov/2018039455

Photo Credits: Getty/Rob Tringali/Sportschrome cover;
Flickr/Keith Allison from Hanover, MD, USA 2, 23;
AP/Matt Slocum 4–5; AP/Tomasso DeRosa 6–7; AP/
Josh Holmberg CALSP 8; Newscom/Cliff Welch/
Icon SMI 10–11; Getty/Alex Trautwig/MLB Photos
12; Newscom/Ray Stubblebine/UPI 15; Getty/
Paul Bereswill 16–17; Getty/Jim McIsaac 18–19;
AP/Christopher Szagola/Cal Sport Media 20

Editors: Wendy Dieker and Alissa Thielges
Designer: Aubrey Harper
Photo Researcher: Holly Young

Printed in the United States of America

HC 10 9 8 7 6 5 4 3 2 1
PB 10 9 8 7 6 5 4 3 2 1

TABLE OF CONTENTS

Power Hitter   5

Sports Star   6

College Years   9

In the Minors   10

Going Pro   13

Tall and Strong   14

In the Outfield   17

The Judge's Chambers   18

A Young Star   21

Just the Facts   22

Words to Know   23

Learn More   24

Index   24

POWER HITTER

Aaron Judge swings the bat. Crack! He smacks the ball. It flies out of the park. Home run! Judge is a pro baseball player. He plays for the New York Yankees.

The first time Judge batted in a pro game, he hit a home run.

SPORTS STAR

Judge grew up in Linden, California. His parents pushed him to work hard. In high school, Judge starred in three sports. Baseball was his favorite.

Growing up, Judge's hero was Rich Aurilia. Aurilia played for the San Francisco Giants.

COLLEGE YEARS

After high school, Judge could have played pro baseball. But he chose to go to college. He went to California State University in Fresno. He played baseball for the Fresno Bulldogs.

IN THE MINORS

In 2013, the New York Yankees **drafted** Judge. He then played in the minor league. He worked on his skills catching the ball. He also worked on hitting the ball.

Judge hit 38 home runs his first year in the minors.

11

GOING PRO

Judge was a **rookie** on the Yankees in 2017. But he was still one of the best hitters. That year he smacked 52 home runs. He won a Rookie of the Year Award.

TALL AND STRONG

Judge is big for a baseball player. He towers over his teammates. His size helped him become a power hitter. But he can also run fast and catch the ball.

Judge stands 6 feet 7 inches (2 m). He weighs about 280 pounds (127 kg).

IN THE OUTFIELD

Judge plays in right field. He is the **outfielder** behind first base. He catches **fly balls**. He also chases after **ground balls**. Then he throws the ball in.

THE JUDGE'S CHAMBERS

Yankee fans have a special cheering section for Judge. It is in the outfield stands. It is called the Judge's Chambers. Fans wear black robes like a court judge.

A YOUNG STAR

Judge continues to knock the ball out of the park. In 2018, he played in the All-Star game. He also hit 27 home runs. He is one of baseball's best young players.

JUST THE FACTS

Born: April 26, 1992

Hometown: Linden, California

College: California State University, Fresno

Joined the majors: 2016

Draft: Round 1, Pick 32

Team: New York Yankees

Position: Outfield

Throws and bats: Right

Stats: www.mlb.com/player/aaron-judge-592450

Accomplishments:

- All-Star Selections: 2018, 2017

- American League Rookie of the Year: 2017

- Silver Slugger: 2017

- Home Run Derby: 2017

WORDS TO KNOW

drafted – to be picked to play for a team

fly ball – when a ball is hit into the air

ground ball – when a ball is hit along the ground

outfielder – a player who is out in the grassy area of the baseball field

rookie – a player in their first year

LEARN MORE

Read More

Fishman, Jon M. *Aaron Judge.* Sports All-Stars. Minneapolis, Minn.: Lerner Publications, 2019.

Flynn, Brendan. *Baseball Time!* Minneapolis: Lerner Publications, 2017.

Websites

ESPN | Aaron Judge
www.espn.com/mlb/player/_/id/33192/aaron-judge

New York Yankees
www.mlb.com/yankees

New York Yankees Kids
www.mlb.com/yankees/fans/kids

INDEX

All-Star game 21
Aurilia, Rich 6
awards 13

college 9

Fresno Bulldogs 9

high school 6, 9
home runs 5, 10, 13, 21

Judge's Chambers 18

minors 10

New York Yankees 5, 10

outfielder 17

parents 6

rookie 13

size 14